UN-DO

YOU NEED DO NOTHING

divinereconnection.com

INTRODUCTION

UN-DO

YOU NEED DO NOTHING

Simple Daily Practices
for *Present Peace* and *Joy*

TYULA ROSE WHITE

DIVINE
RECONNECTION

ISBN: 978-1-3999-5488-4

For you, and for me

and our desire to be free…

Contents

INTRODUCTION

Destination: here, now

Who am I? Why am I here? What is the purpose of this world? Dare we dive into these questions? For many years I tried my best to run away from them, to block them out with any distraction available. But we all have a deep calling to know ourselves fully, and sooner or later we just cannot resist; we must answer this call. You are answering this call right now…

This book is a compilation of pointers that have shown me the way back home. Home to remembering who I really am, why I am really here, and the true purpose of this world. It is my absolute joy to be able to share this with you, so that you, too, may experience the present peace and joy of knowing your true Self.

Largely influenced by the principles of *A Course in Miracles (ACIM)* and other non-dual teachers such as

Eckhart Tolle, Paramhansa Yogananda, David Hoffmeister, Ramana Maharshi, Nisargadatta Maharaj and Mooji, I was inspired to put together a book of daily practices that combine these powerful approaches to Self-realization. Having had many beautiful experiences and revelations through the practice of these teachings, I wanted to create practical ways to easily integrate them into our everyday lives. By truly living them, we open ourselves to receiving more and more miracles each and every day.

A Course in Miracles is a self-study course in mind-training that includes a workbook of 365 daily lessons. These lessons aim to unwind your mind from the ego's thought system of fear, guilt, and lack by removing the obstacles blocking the awareness of love's eternal presence. As a student of the course since 2019, I always found it inspirational to open the book at the beginning of my day and read the practice. Modern life can often feel overwhelming, and this was something that I felt simplified each day by focusing on one lesson like an anchor to draw me back to center throughout any situation.

The phrase, *you need do nothing,* is a line from *A Course in Miracles.* It refers to the fact that your true Self is already perfect. There are no improvements that can be made. It is only the false beliefs about yourself that make you think otherwise. If you did nothing at all, in terms of completely surrendering and letting go of everything — your beliefs, your judgments, trying to understand, trying to control, trying to change what is, and even seeking the truth — the truth will reveal itself. Therefore, what is needed to remember and return to this natural state of mind is an un-doing, an unlearning and releasing of everything you are not, setting your mind free.

I had been diving into the questions of 'the meaning of life' for a good few years before coming to the course, but it wasn't until I started applying the principles of *A Course in Miracles* that my spiritual awakening really kicked in. I began to experience what can only be described as 'the love of God.' There are no words to describe this feeling, but it was like a memory of home, and it came with a bursting desire for everyone else to remember it too. It was like I was overflowing with unconditional love that had to be shared. This sparked my journey into wanting to teach what I had learned.

One evening before giving a talk to a group of friends on choosing Love over fear, I prayed to become a vessel for God and to extend the love I had received. Shortly after, while sitting in meditation, I felt myself being gently lifted from my body. It felt so loving and safe, but the fear of the unknown quickly surfaced, pulling me back again. It was the perfect metaphor for the battle we experience between love and fear.

This was when the real journey through darkness to light began. In the following years, all of the fear, lies, false beliefs, and shadows — anything and everything that had been pushed out of awareness into the dark — had to come up to the surface to be released to the light. I began receiving visions and having mystical experiences that assisted in facing the darkness, letting go of what no longer served and accepting the truth that was being revealed. Honestly, this purification process has been far from easy, but the practice of presence always got me through the darker times, and the space created from releasing all of this is no small gift.

In embracing the process of undoing, and living in presence, I have come to experience the most incredible peace, joy, freedom, and even ecstasy in the simplest of moments. I could just be sitting on the sofa, doing nothing, and the feeling of home comes flooding in. This *knowing* that I am ABSOLUTELY LOVED unconditionally, infinitely, and eternally — and not just loved, but that I am one with that love — I am actually love itself. There is *nothing* I need to do because that is who I am, right now. And the same goes for you. You don't realize how much your thoughts, beliefs, and judgments limit you until you're willing to step outside of them completely.

I am not claiming to be an enlightened being or fully Self-realized, whatever that may mean. For me, this journey feels like an infinite expansion that is not based on reaching a destination, but an ever growing acceptance of the present moment. I am still un-doing! But I am a happy learner, and my perception of life just gets lighter and brighter with increasing peace and joy. Although there may come a time when we are fully aligned with our true Self, allowing it to be revealed naturally is key. It means surrendering and trusting that each moment is unfolding exactly as it is meant to be. The practices I offer you in this book combine presence with shifting your perception, and have been incredible tools in enabling me to experience union with our true nature; the more I practice them, the more integrated these experiences become, and I wish only for you to know this too.

Your own Self-realization
is the greatest service you can render the world
~ Ramana Maharshi ~

Who Am I?
I am pure awareness
This awareness is by its very nature
being, consciousness, bliss (sat-chit-ananda)
~ Ramana Maharshi ~

You need time until you realize, you don't need time
~ Eckhart Tolle ~

Seek not to change the world
but seek to change your mind about the world
~ *A Course in Miracles* ~

You come home when you stop searching
and realize you are already there
~ Blue Marsden ~

WELCOME HOME

Hello You
Welcome home
to your true Self
You have been here before
In fact, you never left
But your memory of this place
has gotten a bit buried
Not to worry… who you *are*
has always been *here*
patiently waiting
to be remembered
Within these pages
are the pointers back home
It's time to find out
who you *really* are.

YOU ARE NOT WHO YOU *THINK* YOU ARE

Who do you think you are?
What if you thought nothing at all…
Who would you be then?

Whether we realize it or not, we tend to spend the majority of our lives in our heads, completely identified with our thoughts. There is a continuous babbling going on. Endless chatter about what we *need* to do, what we *should* have done, and an echo of our beliefs and the stories we've been told. Scenes from the past play over and over like a broken projector. It's completely compulsive, and without our awareness, we mistake these thoughts as facts about who we are.

And what is it that these thoughts are saying to us? That the present moment is not enough… that *we* are not enough. That in order to *be* enough, we must keep *doing* things and chasing goals as a means to somehow improve ourselves. It's almost like a part of us is missing, a feeling of inadequacy that we all feel deep down… and yet, it seems impossible to fill. When we follow these thoughts of lack to do more things, we often start to feel better. And while we *do* achieve momentary satisfaction, this feeling never lasts. No matter what we *do,* it is never enough. We are always left wanting more. And this is because we have been looking in the wrong place entirely.

We think that it’s the *things* of the world that appear outside of us; the relationships, the money, the experiences etc, that will provide us with the love, happiness, and freedom we desire, because they do give us a small taste of these *feelings* — the feeling of being loved, secure and complete. But by being dependent on the things outside to provide what we want to feel inside will never work. We could never be satisfied by the temporary pleasures of the world because what we truly desire is eternal. *We* are eternal. In truth we are not actually lacking anything; it is only our belief that we are that keeps us searching. In forgetting who we are we have lost the connection to our abundance within. So until we decide to look here instead, the cycle continues. We find ourselves stuck in a loop of trying to satisfy a hunger with no end.

The ‘Perfect’ Picture

Most of us were raised with the idea that the purpose of life was to 'grow up,' become somebody, and make something of ourselves. The perfect picture of success usually consists of a steady career, a loving family, a beautiful home, and a flashy car — to work hard until we retire and then die peacefully at an old age. We adopted the thought systems of our parents, our peers, and our cultures. Through these thoughts and beliefs, we created a 'false self,' often suppressing any calls to be different, fearing rejection or abandonment if we dared to step outside the mold. This conditioning creates thoughts that tell us who we are based on what we are *told* rather than what we truly *feel.* But what if we continue to make the same simple mistake…

What if life was not actually about becoming anyone or achieving anything? What if rather than blindly following the production line that keeps us stuck in a wheel of dissatisfaction, we are meant to awaken to our true purpose — to *know* ourselves fully and live in true freedom as who we really are without any expectations of others or fears of not doing or *being* enough. There's nothing we *need* to do but to be present in the only moment there is and experience life to the fullest.

This standard idea of 'life' had often puzzled me; I remember having suspicions from a young age that not all was as it seemed. This was all I had known life to be, but I never quite understood *why* everyone seemed to be getting on with it without question. It was obvious to me that no one here was truly happy, and the things people longed for that they believed would *make* them happy didn't.

Tyula's Turning Point

Part of my story was to fall deeply into the alcohol trap as a means of escaping these seemingly unanswerable questions. It started as a way to 'have fun' and break away from the stress of being a teenager. It gave me a sense of freedom from having to conform in a society that made no sense, as well as within myself, to feel more confident in social situations. It didn't take long before I started to rely on alcohol to provide these things for me. I believed that I couldn't relax, have fun, *be* fun, or even be myself without it. I woke up craving it and passed out, soaked in it. There wasn't an occasion that didn't call for a bottle of wine, be it a kids' party or a job interview.

I grew dependent on it to make me feel full when the reality was it was slowly and very surely breaking me down and ruining my life. When I wasn't drunk, I was in my sick bed and generally had very little energy for anything other than drinking. My only days off were when I physically couldn't hold anything down. Cocaine, marijuana, and sex became common accomplices to my drinking binges. Although it was clear that this behavior was becoming more and more destructive, I had no idea how to stop.

My first attempt to escape this cycle was to decide on having a baby. Although I cut down completely during the pregnancy (bar a few glasses of red wine and half pints of Guinness) once my daughter was born, it wasn't long before I slipped back into the same old ways. This time it seemed much worse as I was trying to escape the responsibilities of being a mother while still having the responsibilities of a mother. Not only was my mind a constant blurry mess, but I would do things that I would never have done had I been sober. I would wake up and have no idea what was a dream and what actually happened, often blacking out completely with whole chunks of time missing from my life. It was a miserable way to live.

It wasn't until I found Allen Carr's *Easyway* that I finally managed to escape the trap. This method became a major key for me in my awakening, in that it not only completely changed my perception of alcohol, but my perception of the world in general. I had believed everything that had been sold to me by society about alcohol; that it was fun, relaxing, freeing, and *normal* to consume poison on a regular basis. And I had used it freely as a way to fulfill my feelings of lack and insecurity, but clearly, it was a complete lie. And this relates to any destructive and addictive distractions presented to us as culture. What they are really there to do is to take our attention away from finding out who we really are and the power that we hold. We don't need anything to complete us. Alcohol, drugs, sex, cigarettes, gambling, gaming, shopping, scrolling, binge-watching, overeating, people pleasing — it's all the same! Chasing illusory highs as a substitute for the most high connection to love that we've forgotten. These things of the world are not *bad* but our attachment to them as a means to distract or define us gives our power away. We try to escape looking within at our own fear and beliefs of unworthiness by keeping our attention outside. We can choose to do this for as long as we want, but essentially we are choosing our suffering, the only way to move away from this darkness is to look within. And it is only here that we begin to find the light that we've been looking for.

I had been numbing myself into a daze nearly every day for ten years straight until I finally reached the point where enough was enough. This was not the way I wanted to continue in this life. I was so done suffering, and it was obvious that I was doing it to myself. It's not an easy step to take that honest look in the mirror at the way our life has gone, but I became so grateful for hitting that rock bottom. It forced me to accept my wake-up call to what was really going on, and offered me the opportunity to learn, grow and share from my experiences. The healing that came from breaking free from this was like a rebirth; I was finally beginning to see things anew. A bitter but necessary medicine, as it readied me to dive into those questions…

There Must Be Another Way

With alcohol no longer being used as a distraction, I finally regained clarity to look at how I had been perceiving the world. The more I began observing the mind and the effects my thoughts had on my experience of 'life,' I began to ask myself… *is* this life? Many of us realize that the pattern of suffering we are often bound in is our own doing and think… *there must be another way*… so we begin seeking answers. I felt called to look into ways of connecting spiritually and find a deeper meaning to life than what I was told.

Being raised in a predominantly atheist environment with little influence from any particular religion or spiritual practices, I was very open to anything. I read many spiritual books, practiced yoga and meditation, worked with plant medicines, spent time in nature, practiced breathwork, worked with energy healing, detoxed from other addictive behaviours and so on. Through these many paths of self-discovery, I experienced some wonderfully enlightening moments, and they did have a massive impact on how I felt and viewed the world, but they often felt very separate and confined to those moments alone. Relaxing and letting go during meditation or in an environment held for the purpose of healing was one thing, but I found that often, as soon as I was away from those spaces and back to my 'normal life,' it felt like nothing had changed. I would find myself distracted, stressed, and overthinking again. And when I faced situations and feelings that I had been trying to let go of, my mind would still be triggered by the same recurring issues. I felt stuck and frustrated. I knew I had to be missing something…

'Spiritual Practice' Is Not Separate From Life. It IS Life.

Although I was becoming very aware that all this overthinking and restlessness was distracting me from getting to the core of my problems, modern life didn't allow for much quiet reflection. At least not the amount that I felt was necessary to be able to focus on the inner work needed to truly free my mind. As a busy mother of two, I found it was quite unrealistic to just stop doing things, and it was usually the last thing on my list of things to do. This is something I found most frustrating on my healing journey. I would notice an irritation within me when I didn't have enough time to spend on my own well-being and was even resentful of the responsibilities of life, taking up the time that I could be spending 'in peace.'

One evening, as I was putting my son to sleep (which always seemed to be a long, drawn-out affair), I found myself praying for patience. Suddenly a memory came to me about prayer. That when you pray for something, what you receive is the opportunity to practice it. There I was, praying for something that was literally right there for me to *be*, and something just clicked. I realized this had been *begging* for my attention, and it was now so clearly in front of me. I finally came to accept what I had been avoiding all along — the present moment. I had wanted to run away from the stresses of life and what seemed to be the difficult parts so that I could just relax, when I could practice relaxing *right now*. The peace I had been seeking was within me. I just needed to be present for it.

We are not our life story; we are the life behind the story. The Spirit that is forever free. But when we get so caught up in the story, and place our peace in a non-existent future scenario, we are continuously drawn away from our center of simply *being,* and the wonderful gifts that are inherently *given now.*

Spiritual practice is not separate from life. It *is* life. In fact, nothing is separate. But by keeping my life and my spirituality separate in my mind, I had struggled to feel the peace and joy I would experience in those moments of feeling connected to spirit in my everyday life. My desire to escape my triggers and block them out by sitting in meditation was not encouraging any real transformation. Seated meditation is a powerful practice to have, but in preparation to face life, not escape it. Integration is a must.

TWO CHOICES

The Ego

To find out who you are
You must first recognize
Who you are not

Imagine the reality you are currently experiencing, like watching a movie. The scenes you see as outside of yourself are a projection of your inner thought system. As your light of awareness shines through all of these thoughts, beliefs, and conditioning built up over lifetimes, they act as filters that, combined, make up your own perception of the world.

Essentially, when we look out onto the world through these filters, we are not seeing the truth. Our perception is separate and, therefore, distorted. If everyone sees the same world differently, how can we say what is true? Without a higher viewpoint, we tend to believe that what we *see* is who we are. Like clouds casting shadows over our true identity, this can feel dark and lonely. It causes us to believe we have separated from the whole, perpetuating a thought system of fear, lack, shame, and guilt. This false idea about ourselves is the personality self, the ego.

So how did this happen? Imagine that all is mind. Everything that exists is within the one mind of God, so what we are experiencing here in this physical plane of time and space is *'a tiny, mad idea' (ACIM)* that we could be separate. By believing in this idea, there no longer seems to be one but *two*, and the result is the projected world of duality. We believe that who we *are* is a separate body with separate goals and interests; a separate being that is born and dies. This idea is a fearful one and is the reason that we experience so much suffering as we resist and project out our fear thoughts and feelings of guilt for what we think we have done. But that is exactly what it is, just a fearful idea that keeps playing out on loop until we choose to let it go. It could never be true. The mind, however, is very powerful, and as I said, what we believe is real will appear very real to us in our 'external world'.

Our mind appears split, caught up somewhere between fear and love, ego and spirit. This conflict appears to us everywhere. We rejects parts of ourselves and cast them outside, throwing out what we don't want so that it's not us; it's them. But really, it's our own self-hatred for believing we are who we are not. The more we listen to our ego thoughts the more we are feeding them and allowing them to have a greater hold over us. The purpose of meditation; be it seated or continued throughout our day with practices like the ones in this book, is to offer up all of these fear thoughts. Doubt thoughts, judgements, grievances, beliefs, opinions, and concepts, all of these seemingly separate things that are actually all just one giant fog of nothingness that keeps us distracted and blocks our awareness of the truth. The only way to see the ego for what it is, is to undo all of this conditioning and return to the unconditioned mind.

The ego only appears to exist in linear time, so when we constantly live our lives in terms of past and future, the ego remains. It will encourage us to hold on to past experiences, proclaiming that by doing so, it is keeping us 'safe' so that we don't make the same mistakes again in future. But when we hold on to the past, the future becomes a projection based on it. We subconsciously wish we could change things and do things differently so the past repeats for us. When holding on to these memories of how things played out last time, we recreate the same experiences, and round and round we go. Within this cycle, we remain asleep, like a veil of amnesia that leaves us blind to the eternal presence of spirit where we would know true happiness. But because we have become so accustomed to this way of living, we tend to experience massive resistance to the present moment, often avoiding it at all costs with all kinds of distractions. Take a moment to pause in presence, and notice how long it takes before you start to become restless. This is the pull of the ego.

The ego works in a way of, *if this, then that*, and places conditions on your happiness. For example:

If you work hard enough, *then* you will be successful.
If you accumulate enough money and things, *then* you will be content.
If you look a certain way, *then* you will be accepted.
If you are nice enough, *then* you will be loved.
If you meditate long enough, *then* you will reach enlightenment.
If you do enough good deeds, *then* you will go to heaven.

It's a trick, and it keeps you bound in a loop of searching for something that you *already* are. 'Seek but do not find' is the mantra of the ego because there is no *then*, there is only now, and you are *already* a success. You are *already* accepted, and you are *already* loved. You are already everything that you need to be, there are no conditions that you need to meet because it is all within you now.

The Alternative

Know that all that you are can never be undone
What you think you've done, you never did
What is true can never change
And what you are, is the truth

Although we have long believed the impossible to be what is real, we are constantly being called back home to truth. Our true nature is of Spirit, with the ego being the false personal self, the illusion. The voice for God, the Holy Spirit is given as the correction for the error of this belief. In quieting our minds from the loud and fearful cries of the ego we can begin to hear the gentle whispers to return to love. The only mistake we ever made was choosing to believe in the ego. We chose time over eternity, but instead of remaining bound to it, we can instead use time as a learning tool to guide us back home. Although it may sound like I have referred to the ego as if it is an actual entity that lives in pursuit of deceiving us, let me reiterate the entire ego thought-system is a mistaken, fearful belief. An idea in the mind that, when given our energy and attention, becomes the illusory world we experience. The emptiness we feel is not true, but an imagining resulting from our belief in separation. We chose to put our trust in it, without realizing it was a lie, but now that we know, we can choose again. Not as a means to make anything better or different in the world, but by choosing to make a higher-level choice — to transcend the ego completely by letting it go.

Because we have identified with the ego for so long, it's not easy to just switch it off. Letting go of who we thought we were is a kind of death, so it's not surprising that we can find it difficult to accept this process. The ego identity would much prefer that we continue to believe in our separateness, because if we were to discover that this separation never actually occurred —that it was only our belief in it that made it seem real — then that would mean that the ego in truth, never really existed. It was all a dream.

Discovering that beneath all of our beliefs and conditioning, under all of the 'shoulds' and 'should nots,' buried by the constant thoughts of 'if only' and 'I wish,' is everything you have always longed for. Love. Acceptance. Freedom. When we allow these filters to fall away, we begin to see. Beyond the shadows and behind the clouds, the light of who we are still shines just as bright. One, eternal, beautiful light. Bliss, joy, ecstasy. Holy, pure, and innocent. Always right *here* for us to come home to.

I have used the word God in this book, some call this The Universe, The Divine, The Light, Oneness, Brahman, Source; they are all symbolic of the same term for the source of all life, all that is. The Holy Spirit is just one name for the voice for God, the bridge home that never leaves us comfortless. This may also be called your higher Self, your intuition, your inner voice, Christ consciousness, Jesus Christ, your spirit guides. Any name is welcome and will assist you in rising up on your journey should you call for help. Whenever I find myself in distress, I pray to the Holy Spirit or Jesus, *'please let me see things differently'* and my perception often shifts immediately. Have faith that you have been heard and be open to receiving the correction. Heaven, nirvana and bliss are all states of mind that can be experienced when our minds are completely unclouded. In handing over everything that blocks this awareness we return to our true nature. *You need do nothing*, but allow it to be revealed.

The ego is not your enemy; it is merely a role you have been playing that you mistook for who you are.

There is no need to battle a shadow, as there is no reason to fear an illusion. We can use what the ego has made as a teaching tool to recognize the true from the false. When we bring these shadows to the light, we can see them for what they are. What happens when you shine a light on a shadow?

We are constantly presented with opportunities to undo the ego's thought-system. Whatever draws us out of our peace *is* our inner work to heal. We just need to listen. Allow our attention and awareness to rest in the present moment, without becoming distracted by our thoughts and judgments, and realize what life is trying to teach us. Every moment is an offering to choose again. To forgive the past, to let go of *everything* we think we know, and let the light in. The universe speaks to us, providing reflections of our beliefs and pointers to show us the way home to our true selves. We are not separate from life, we are life! And when we begin to see everything as a whole, we begin to feel that wholeness within that we have been searching for all along. We can step out of the ego game and live freely in our truth.

ABOUT THE PRACTICES

We are creating space for revelation
To be in that timeless moment in time
The instant to remember who we really are
With a clear mind
We make room for the Divine

These practices are designed to run throughout your day and be integrated into your current lifestyle. They are universal; it doesn't matter whether you are completely new to spiritual practice or have already worked with many. Your religion, race, age, sex, or any other labels and false limits are irrelevant. Our essence is the same, and this is the realization we aim to come to in taking on these practices. In accepting our shared purpose to know ourselves fully, we are doing our part to heal the whole idea of separation in the collective mind.

You are invited to take on these practices daily until presence becomes your nature again. All you need to begin these practices is a little willingness to see things differently. Words are symbolic and cannot express what lies beyond; only in your choice to remember will you experience this for yourself. With dedication each day to one of these simple practices, you will begin to expand your consciousness beyond anything you can imagine. The seeming obstacles that are keeping you from the awareness of love's infinite presence will begin to melt away, and your eternal inner peace will grow ever more apparent.

Life *can* be simple when you live it moment by moment, and joyfully embrace that the only time is now. These practices will free up your mind to surrender and accept life. This is a way of being which can be brought about by combining our spiritual practices with our daily life and seeing them as one. By bringing awareness and space into our busy lives, we can shift our consciousness into a more connected state where we no longer feel lost, depressed, and anxious, but free, full, and held by the light. Allow the softness of divine grace to shine through, and the flow and harmony of your journey here will naturally unfold before you. The path to Self-realization is within you.

We will be practicing how to connect with our still center. This inner peace can be found in whatever you do and wherever you are. There is no need to continuously attend retreats or sit for hours in meditation; you can be in this inner space anytime and anywhere. A regular seated meditation practice is beneficial to finding stillness and inner space, and you can use these practices as prompts for longer meditation sessions, but the main objective of this book is to develop the ability to connect to your being, throughout your doing. Embrace meditation in your movement as a continuous mindful way to truly live your life.

There are many spiritual practices that exist, and there is no right or wrong way to make this return home; they will all lead you to the same place eventually. But for me, practicing presence has been the greatest miracle I could have asked for. Some practices out there can feel quite complex or confusing or require you to make seemingly drastic changes to your lifestyle, but presence is simple. It is never about *what* you are doing at the time, but the feeling of present peace, love, and joy within.

Although presence is simple, that does not mean it is always easy. Maintaining presence takes dedication, as it can be a challenge for the mind that is not used to this way of being. You may experience momentary glimpses of a heavenly state, but it is very easy for the mind to slip back into what it is used to, which is exactly why I decided to develop these daily practices — with the word *practice* emphasized here. Within these pages are 33 simple keys that allow you to connect within, no matter what you're doing, along with helpful ways to remind you throughout the day, making it possible to integrate spiritual practice into your everyday life with greater ease.

You are likely to experience some resistance to the continuation of these practices as you loosen the ego's grip, but do not let this stop you. Notice your resistance and hold it in the spaciousness of love without judgment. There may be times when you feel like you are losing your mind, but this is often a necessary step in setting it free. Be gentle with yourself as you go through this process of un-doing, and don’t worry if it ever feels like you are going backwards; you are on the right path. There is a reason you are reading this book now. You are being called to let go and return home. Return to peace, return to love. Allow yourself to hear the whispers of your heart and let the glimpses of the truth that come spur you onwards. Know that you are giving up nothing and receiving everything. The more you practice anchoring the truth, whilst simultaneously releasing the false, the more natural this will become as you continuously reinforce your choice for peace. The greatest gift you could ever give yourself.

What you are seeking is never outside of you, but literally… *is you.* You couldn't be any closer to the truth, but this is for you to discover for yourself. Experiencing this for yourself is key to your own liberation, which is why this book is not meant to increase your knowledge but is a means to reveal your inner wisdom. All you need is to be willing to un-do what you think you know and allow yourself to reconnect to the truth. True peace and joy is awaiting you now.

How to UN-DO

Initially, I suggest that these practices are taken on in the order they are presented. Once you have experienced each one of them, I invite you to approach this book like an Oracle. Feel into your heart-center, take a deep breath, and open the book at random to your practice for the day. Trust that whatever shows up is what is meant for you in this now moment.

Alternatively, if you find yourself drawn to a particular practice you wish to stick with, continue with the same one for as long as you like. Follow your intuition to find what works best for you.
If you fully surrender to just one of these practices, you will have mastered them all. This is not a cumulative course but many pointers to the same truth. There is only one. And you are it.

Integrating These Practices Into Your Everyday

1. Find a quiet space to read through the practice at the beginning of the day and sit with it for at least five minutes (more is welcome).

2. Set the intention that your practice is the most important thing that you do today.

3. Set the practice symbol as your screensaver /wallpaper to serve as a reminder. (Scan QR

code found in the back of this book for downloadable images)

4. Take a photo of the practice text to have it with you if you'd like to refer back to it later.

5. Set phone reminders to notify you throughout the day. You can use the quotes for added impact. You could also put post-it notes around your home or workplace for an extra boost!

6. Repeat the practice subtitle in your mind as often as possible throughout the day. Some will be more of a mantra to be mentally repeated; others are action-words like *watch* or *listen.* (you can do this with eyes closed too whenever feels appropriate)

7. Put the principle into practice as often as you can, don't worry if you forget, you can always remember again.

8. End your day with quiet contemplation of the day's practice before bed, or integrate it into your evening meditation practice.

YOU NEED DO NOTHING

to be loved
to be complete
to be accepted
to be whole
to be joyful
to be at peace
to be happy
to be free
to be valued
to be enough
to be a success
to be your Self
to be

The saying 'you need do nothing' is not the same as, 'don't do anything,' but instead means there is nothing you *need* to do in order to be loved, to be worthy, or to *be* who you *are*. It is helpful to allow yourself to do nothing to connect to the part of you that knows this. The part of you that is usually masked by the ego's voice that constantly says you are not enough, that you must keep *doing* to be worthy, and realize there was never anything outside of you or in the future that could ever be gained. The truth is, there is only ever *now,* and there is only ever one. You already are everything, and there is nothing you need to do in order to be your Self. You are loving awareness, and love does not *do* anything; it just is.

When you truly drop into your being, inspiration will arise. It may be something unexpected that you wouldn't usually allow yourself to do but trust in those nudges; this will lead to inspired action. The 'doing' that arises from this place of being will be in alignment with your true Self, an extension of the love and joy that you *are* rather than that of society's expectations and the ego's fearful beliefs.

You need do nothing is the beginning and the end; the full circle. We begin with this practice as a means to set the scene, but it is also the end goal realisation. Keep this in mind as you journey through all of the practices that reconnect you to your being. There is a truth in you that can never change. You are already home. You are already perfect. And you can know this freedom right here and now, in the present moment. Presence *is* Love. Love is here.

THE PRACTICES

You Need Do Nothing

'I need do nothing'

1

You Need Do Nothing

'I need do nothing'

Allow yourself to do nothing
Let your mind and body completely relax
Drop your jaw, relax your shoulders
take a deep breath into your belly... and release
Allow any plans or responsibilities
to gently melt away

Notice what your mind says
when you try and do this
Often it will search frantically
for things you *need* to do
reasons why you can't possibly 'do nothing'
there is so much to do…
Allow these thoughts to pass you by

There is always something that says it needs doing
but there is no need to follow these thoughts
no matter how urgent they appear
they are not true… do no-thing…

In this space of relaxation, become aware
of the part of you that always does nothing
The still center of your being
The presence beneath the thoughts
The changeless awareness
from which all is simply observed
When you know yourself as this perfect stillness
you realize *you* are never actually doing anything

You need do nothing
As your body seems to be going about
doing things today
simply observe from the stillness of your center
Notice the way life goes on
without your conscious effort
Knowing there is no need to push the river
enter into a state of flow
and repeat these words…
'I Need Do Nothing'

~

When the goal is finally achieved by anyone
it always comes with just one happy realization
"I need do nothing"
~
This quiet center, in which you do nothing,
will remain with you
giving you rest in the midst of every busy doing
on which you are sent
~ *A Course in Miracles* ~

Nothing outside yourself can cause any trouble
you yourself make the waves in your mind
If you leave your mind as it is,
it will become calm
This mind is called big mind
~ Shunryu Suzuki ~

YOU NEED DO NOTHING

I NEED DO NOTHING

Observe Your Thoughts

Watch

2

Observe your Thoughts

Watch

Today we will observe our thoughts
without judgment
Take a moment to pause
and simply become aware
that thinking is happening
Notice the thoughts as they come and go

Now as you watch your thoughts, contemplate;
Who is it that is watching these thoughts?
If it is I that can watch these thoughts
then these thoughts cannot be me
Stay with the I that is watching
as you do so, you loosen the identification
of these thoughts as being who you are

Notice the kind of thoughts that come up
Observe how they make you feel
Is it a loving thought or a fearful one?
If it is not love, see it as a call for love
and a call to let it go
This is a process
of sorting the true from the false

Physically relax your brain
release your forehead and any tension behind the eyes
unclench your jaw, and soften

Choose not to feed these thoughts

with any further contemplation
allowing them to drift by
like clouds in the sky
Noticing too the space in between the clouds
gradually clearing the way for the light to shine

Allow this awareness to run throughout your day
Notice how often these thoughts take you away
from the present moment
You are not your thoughts

~

Observe your thoughts, don't believe them
~ Eckhart Tolle ~

Consciousness is observing your thoughts and action
so that you can live from true choice
in the present moment
rather than being run by programming from the past
~ T Harv Eker ~

The moment you realize you are not present
you are present
Whenever you can observe your mind,
you are no longer trapped in it
~ Eckhart Tolle ~

Is it true? Can you absolutely know that it's true?
How do you react when you believe that thought?
Who would you be without the thought?
~ Byron Katie ~

OBSERVE YOUR THOUGHTS

WATCH WATCH WATCH

Notice the Breath

(Inhale) Peace, (Exhale) Release

3

Notice the Breath

(Inhale) Peace, (Exhale) Release

Bring your awareness to the breath
Feel the rhythm as you inhale… and exhale
Resist the desire to control it
and just observe the gentle rise and fall
that is flowing through without effort

Observe how the cool air feels on an inhale
breathing in present peace
Feel the subtle warmth of the air on an exhale
breathing out a softening release

Remain in this awareness of the breath
throughout the day
Notice, without judgment
the slight changes that occur
when in different situations

If you experience yourself as stressed or anxious
take a few deep cleansing breaths into your belly
In through your nose… out through your nose
hold for a count of three, and repeat
Inhale peace… exhale release
Watch your breath as it settles back
to its natural rhythm

Allow the breath to be the focus of your day
Let it be your anchor
that returns you safely home

to the present moment
where life is breathed through you
Inhale peace… exhale release

~

Breathing in, there is only the present moment.
Breathing out, it is a wonderful moment
~
Breathing in, I calm the body and mind
Breathing out, I smile
Dwelling in the present moment
I know this is the only moment
~
Breath is the bridge that connects life to consciousness
which unites your body with your thoughts
Whenever your mind becomes scattered
use your breath
as a means to take hold of your mind again

~ Thich Nhat Hanh ~

NOTICE THE BREATH

INHALE PEACE EXHALE RELEASE

Relax and Release

'I choose to let go'

4

Relax and Release

'I choose to let go'

Holding creates blocks in the natural flow of life
Holding on to the past, to beliefs and trauma
reflects in our holding of tension in the body
Instead of holding on today
we will choose to let go

By observing the body
as a reflection of our mental resistance
tune into any tension, discomfort, or dis-ease
Breathe into the area or feeling
that you are observing
and consciously relax and release it on an exhale
Allow your body to move or shake if it feels good

Continue this throughout your day
Noticing as and when tension arises
stay vigilant for any moments
that you are drawn out of your peace
When you experience strong emotions
notice how they feel in the body
and consciously direct your energy
into relaxing and releasing
No need to question or judge these feelings
Just notice, feel them
and choose to let go

There may be certain areas
that regularly tense back up

check back there often
and consciously relax

Give thanks for all opportunities to let go now
Instead of holding on to conflict
retrain yourself to be centered and at peace
in any circumstance
surrendering to all that is
and repeat this phrase to yourself
'I choose to let go'

~

Relax your shoulders and relax your heart
Let go and give room for the pain
to pass through you
It's just energy
Just see it as energy and let it go

~

I am so grateful that surrender has taught me
to willingly participate in life's dance
with a quiet mind and an open heart
~ Michael A. Singer ~

Honor your being
release each and every struggle
gather strength from life's storms
relax into the arms of spirit
~ Jonathan Lockwood Huie ~

RELAX AND RELEASE

I CHOOSE TO LET GO

Feel the Life Within

Feel

5

Feel the Life Within

Feel

When you close your eyes
are you aware of your body still being there?

Tune into the feeling of aliveness
that is flowing through your entire being
Draw your awareness away from the five senses
and see if you can turn your attention inward
to the life force that comes before them

Give yourself time to really drop in
and feel every tingle
every cell vibrating
the subtle energy of life that moves through you
surrounding you at every moment

Do you notice it more intensely in certain areas?
If so, bring your attention
to where it is less obvious too
Be curious as you observe
the sensations of your inner space
Releasing any thoughts or judgments and just feeling

As often as possible throughout your day today
draw your attention away from your thoughts
and into the feeling of life within you
Where your attention goes, energy flows
You *are* life

The truth is you don't have a life; you are life

~

Spiritual awakening is becoming awake
to the aliveness of this very moment

~

Awareness of the inner body
is consciousness remembering its origin
and returning to source

~

Body awareness not only anchors you
in the present moment
it is a doorway out of the prison that is the ego
It also strengthens the immune system
and the body's ability to heal itself

~ Eckhart Tolle ~

FEEL THE LIFE WITHIN

FEEL FEEL FEEL

Listen to the Silence

Listen

6

Listen to the Silence

Listen

Beneath the noise, there is always silence
Beneath the motion, there is always stillness
The constant foundation of all that is

With change as the only certainty in this world
how does this changeless place feel?

If the truth cannot change,
you may ask yourself
What is really real?
What is changeless in you?

Notice when you are in a state of listening
are you thinking?
Listen
No matter how much noise
there seems to be around you today
Come back to the silence of the mind
when you are listening

To listen to the silence, wherever you are
is an easy and direct way of becoming present
Even if there is noise, there is always some silence
underneath and in between the sounds
Listening to the silence immediately creates stillness
inside you
~
Pay more attention to the silence than the sounds
Paying attention to outer silence creates inner silence
The mind becomes still. A portal is opening up
~ Eckhart Tolle ~

Listen to the wind, it talks
Listen to the silence, it speaks
Listen to your heart, it knows
~ Native American Proverb ~

There is a voice that doesn't use words
Listen
~
Listen to silence, it has so much to say
~ Rumi ~

LISTEN TO THE SILENCE

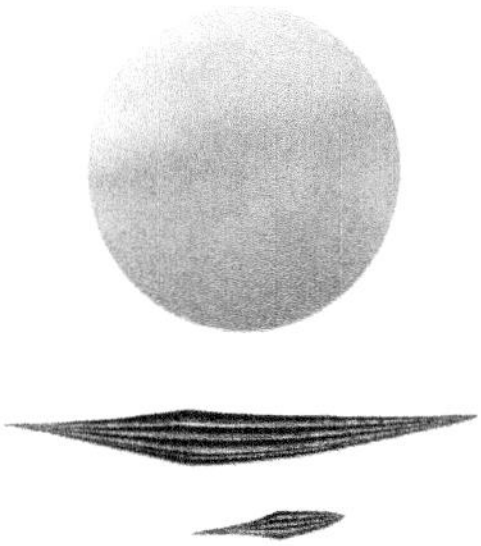

LISTEN LISTEN LISTEN

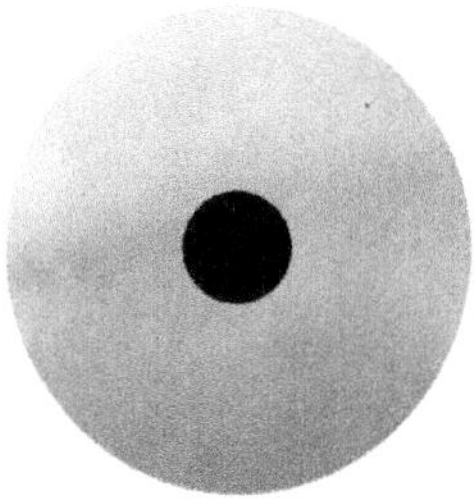

Connect to the Stillness

Be still

7

Connect to the Stillness

Be still

On the surface
life can often feel wild and manic
with everything in constant motion
and ever-changing
But just as the waves on a stormy sea
crash about wildly from above
in the depths of the ocean, all is calm
all is still
There is no knowledge of the mayhem above
Today we will dwell in this stillness

Notice this stillness in nature
As you look at a plant, it is completely still
Even if it is blowing in the wind
there is a stillness
Unwavering
Unaffected by the external
Feel that stillness within yourself
Within your center
there is a perfect, brilliant stillness
A place that never changes
never moves
When you feel overwhelmed
by what appears to you externally
remember, and come home to this place
Be still

As you rest into stillness, more profoundly
awareness becomes free of the minds compulsive
control, contractions and identifications
Awareness naturally returns to its non-state of
absolute un-manifest potential
The silent abyss beyond all knowing
~ Adyashanti ~

Within you, there is a stillness and a sanctuary
To which you can retreat at any time and be yourself
~ Hermann Hesse ~

In the stillness of the mind, I saw myself as I am —
unbound
~ Nisargadatta Maharaj ~

Wisdom comes with the ability to be still
Just look and listen, no more is needed
Being still, looking, and listening activates the
non-conceptual intelligence within you
Let stillness direct your words and actions
~ Eckhart Tolle ~

Be still and know that I Am God
~ Psalm 46:10 ~

CONNECT TO THE STILLNESS

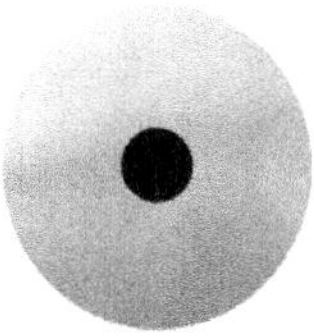

BE STILL

BE STILL

Feel the Space

Expand

8

Feel the Space

Expand

Look around you
What do you see?
People, plants, objects, buildings…
What about the space in between?
Have you ever given your attention
to the room within the room?
The air that surrounds you
the infinite space when you look at the sky?

This spaciousness is also within you
You and this space are one
in a unified embrace of Love
Feel the expanse through your heart space
There are no boundaries
no separation between your body and the air
When you walk outside today
feel as if the breeze is flowing through you
connecting you to all that is
There is no other

Feel into this space as often as possible today
tuning in to the un-manifest
the vast expansiveness of the unseen
the boundless sea of light that embraces us all
Play with it with your hands
Dance with it
How does it feel?
How do you feel?

Hold all that you see and don't see
within this infinite space
cast nothing outside
for all is one
and all is you

~

You can't feel the earth if you can't feel the space
~ Chogyam Trungpa ~

That stillness and vastness
that enables the universe to be
is not just out there in space…
it is also within you
~
Presence is a state of inner spaciousness
~ Eckhart Tolle ~

Where do I begin and end in space?
I have relations to the sun and air
which are just as vital parts of existence
as my heart
~ Alan Watts ~

The wondrous beauty of life
is forever held in Love's embrace
~ Harold W. Becker ~

FEEL THE SPACE
EXPAND EXPAND

Stay with the Observer

Watch

9

Stay with the Observer

Watch

As you go about your day
experiencing your world
pay attention
Whatever you can observe, is not you
So who are you?
Where are you?
Who is looking through your eyes?
Who is feeling through your hands?
Notice the awareness that is always there
Conscious, present, loving awareness
Be with the one who is watching

Observe the scenes that appear before you
without judgment or attachment
When you remain in this simple state of awareness
notice how you experience things differently
How does the world look to you now?
How do you feel?

Whenever you are drawn out of this presence
remember that you are not what you see
The past is just replaying for you to let it go
So let it go
Soften your gaze
and enjoy the movie
You are loving awareness

To know yourself as the being underneath the thinker
the stillness underneath the mental noise
the love and joy underneath the pain
is freedom, salvation, enlightenment
~ Eckhart Tolle ~

Observe 'What is' with undivided awareness
~ Bruce Lee ~

Observe, and in the observation, there is
neither the "observer' nor the 'observed'
— there is only observation taking place
~
The observer is the observed
~ Jiddu Krishnamurti ~

Sometimes it is the quiet observer
who sees the most
~ Katherine L. Nelson ~

STAY WITH THE OBSERVER

WATCH WATCH WATCH

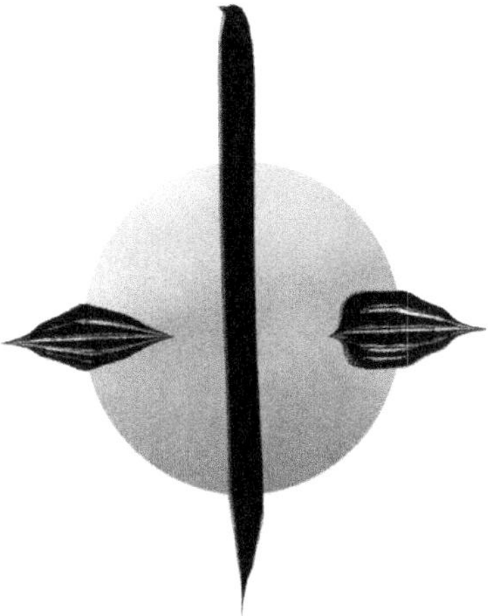

Focus on One Thing at a Time

Focus

10

Focus on One Thing at a Time

Focus

Do you often find yourself jumping
from one thing to the next
getting distracted
and even forgetting what you were doing?
Today we will slow down

Focus your mind
on doing just one thing at a time
Offer your full attention to whatever you are doing
observing with curiosity and care
Allow the energy of your entire being
to be in this moment only

Notice when your mind wants to jump ahead
to what is coming next
and gently guide your attention back
to the present moment
Nothing else matters
other than what you are doing now
Whatever you are doing, be there completely
Where possible
always finish what you are doing
before moving on to something else
No multitasking allowed

If you find yourself getting frustrated
or judging yourself
Breathe, release, and try again

Zen teaches you to pay attention to every detail
Immersing yourself in your activity to such a degree
that you become the activity
~ Gary R. ~

Do one thing at a time, and while doing it
put your whole soul into it, to the exclusion of all else
~ Swami Vivekananda ~

The only thing that is ultimately real about your
journey is the step that you are taking at this moment
That's all there ever is
~ Eckhart Tolle ~

Until my ONE thing is done
everything else is a distraction
~ Gary W. Keller ~

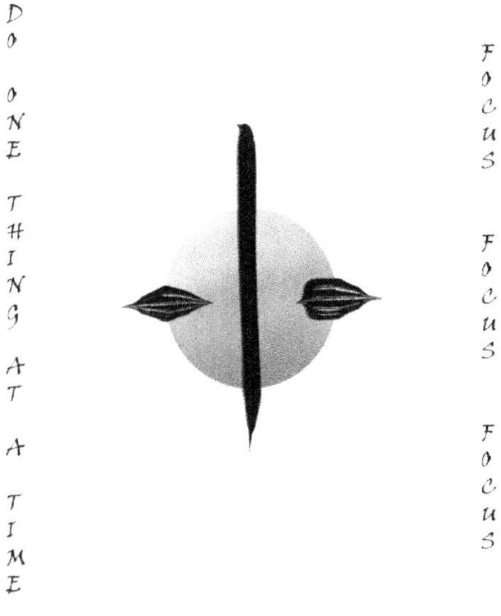
DO ONE THING AT A TIME
FOCUS FOCUS FOCUS

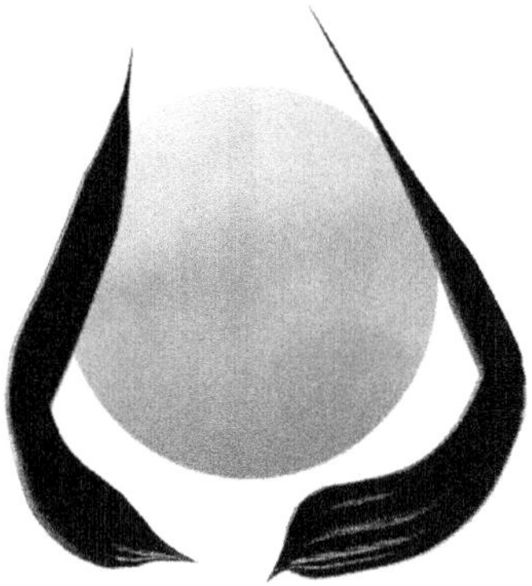

Do Everything with Love

'I love you'

11

Do Everything with Love

'I love you'

Whether you are washing your face
or a pile of dirty plates
making your breakfast
or taking out the bins
do everything
with exactly the same amount
of love and care
Feel the love that you are
extending in every moment
Treat everyone and everything
as you would like to be treated
If anything seems to be unlike love
see it as a call for love
and respond with love
Allow your thoughts, words, and actions
to align in the frequency of love
pouring your heart into everything you do
cultivating unconditional love
for the present moment

Notice how your judgments change
when you begin to hold every little thing
within the same respect
in love's embrace

Open your heart and become devotion in motion
Repeating this mantra throughout your day
'I love you… I love you… I love you'

What is done in love is done well
~ Vincent Van Gogh ~

Do everything with so much love in your heart,
that you would never want to do it any other way
~ Yogi Desai ~

Do everything in Love
~ Corinthians 16:14 ~

Let everything we do and say
be an expression of the beauty in our heart
always based on Love
~ Don Miguel Ruiz ~

Eventually, you will come to understand
that Love heals everything, and love is all there is
~ Gary Zukav ~

DO EVERYTHING WITH LOVE

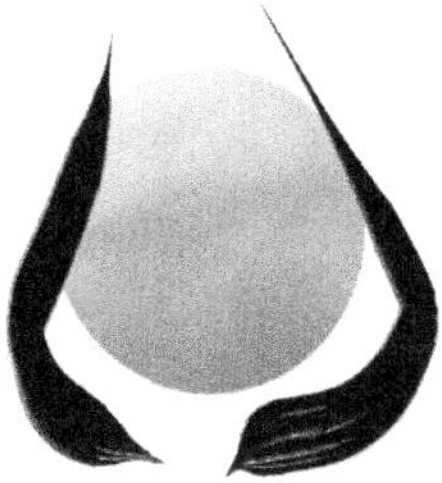

I LOVE YOU I LOVE YOU

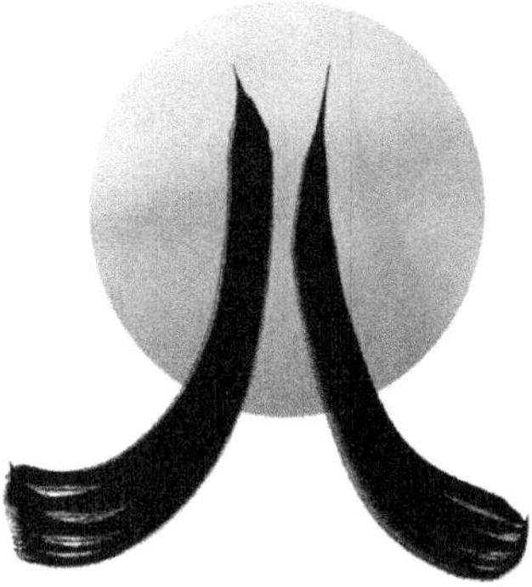

Say Thank You!

'Thank you, thank you, thank you'

12

Say Thank You!

'Thank you, thank you, thank you'

Thank you is your mantra today
Thank everything and everyone you see
Thank every situation
every thought and every feeling
Everything is equally worthy
of your gratitude
Say it out loud
repeat it in your head
feel the frequency of gratitude
in everything you do

Notice your resistance to thank certain things
and try to release your judgments
Give equal thanks to all

Begin to see everything
through the same loving eyes
revealing life's unity
Oneness
Thank you, thank you, thank you

It is through gratitude for the present moment
that the spiritual dimension of life opens up
~ Eckhart Tolle ~

If the only prayer you ever say
in your entire life is thank you
it will be enough
~ Meister Eckhart ~

Gratitude is the greatest prayer
Thank you is the greatest mantra
~ Swami Nithyananda ~

Your mantra is thank you
Just keep saying thank you
Don't explain. Don't complain. Just say thank you
Say thank you for existence
~ Mooji ~

SAY THANK YOU
THANK YOU

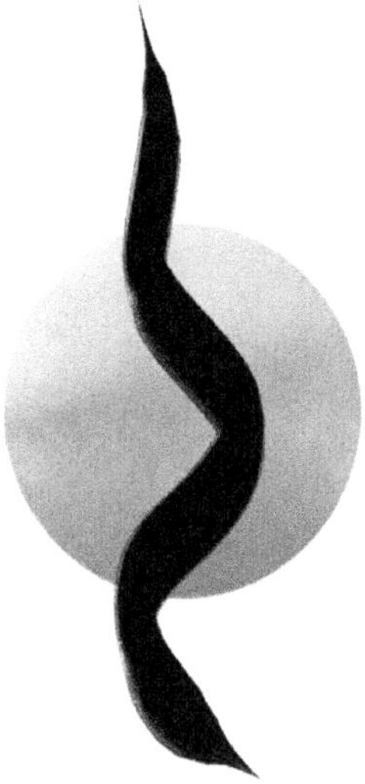

Flow Like Water

Soften

13

Flow Like Water

Soften

Notice how you are moving through this world
How do you handle the challenges that arise?
Do you accept what happens without judgment
or resist and push to change what is?
Does your experience of the world
feel hard and rigid
or soft and fluid?

Imagine that you are water
How would you navigate your day?
Feel the softness in all you see
Accept and flow through any situation
let things come, and let them go

You are part of the flow of life
you can choose to resist it
allowing fear and judgment to hold you back
or travel along with it
inviting in ease and love for the journey

There is no need to push the river
Release the need to control the uncontrollable
and surrender to what life has to offer you
Softly flowing as you go

Empty your mind, be formless, shapeless, like water
You put water in a cup it becomes the cup
You put water in a bottle it becomes the bottle
You put water into a teapot it becomes the teapot
Now water can flow, or it can crash
Be water, my friend
~
Running water never grows stale,
So you have to just keep on flowing
~ Bruce Lee ~

The wave does not need to die to become water
She is already water
~ Thich Nhat Hanh ~

Nothing is softer or more flexible than water
yet nothing can resist it
~ Lao Tzu ~

You can't stop the wave, but you can learn to surf
~ Joseph Goldstein ~

FLOW LIKE WATER
SOFTEN SOFTEN

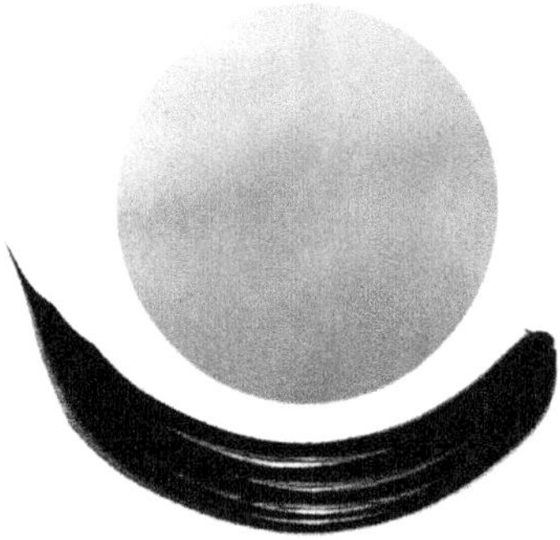

Wait for your Beloved

Quiet anticipation

14

Wait for Your Beloved

Quiet anticipation

Today we will indulge in a little role play
Imagine you are awaiting your beloved's arrival home
They could come at any time
and you want to hear them when they do
so that you may greet them at the door

As you go about your day,
listen intently for the arrival of your beloved
Be silent in all of your activities
moving quietly and with care
Imagine that all that you do today
is in loving anticipation of their return

Notice if you take on a fearful
or anxious disposition in playing this role
and know that there is nothing to fear
You are very much looking forward to their arrival
Your beloved loves you unconditionally
and will come without judgment
You simply desire
to show them your love in return

A state of peaceful alertness
is the intention of today

The world is full of magic things
Patiently waiting for our senses to grow sharper
~ W.B. Yeats ~

Patience is not the ability to wait
but the ability to keep a good attitude while waiting
~ Joyce Meyer ~

Waiting time is not wasted time
Waiting patiently in expectation
is the foundation of the spiritual life
~ Henri Nouwen ~

Trust the wait, embrace the uncertainty
Enjoy the beauty of becoming
When nothing is certain, anything is possible
~ Mandy Hale ~

Infinite patience brings immediate results
~ *A Course in Miracles* ~

WAIT FOR YOUR BELOVED
QUIET ANTICIPATION

Judge Nothing

'I am neutral'

15

Judge Nothing

'I am neutral'

As you observe your surroundings
notice how you are judging all that you see
Past learning and experiences
are projected onto the world
Things are labeled good or bad…
beautiful, ugly, and so on

For example: Look at a pen
You have a name for it
you learned of its function
you have memories of how it feels in your hand
the times in which you have used it
the way it writes
the materials of which it is made, and so on
You're not really seeing the pen as it is

Take a deep breath
close your eyes for a moment
then take a look at the pen again with fresh eyes
Try not to label anything about it and just observe
as if you had never seen it before
What do you see now?
In releasing judgment, you are setting it free
allowing yourself to see everything exactly as it is
Innocent

Continue this throughout your day
Include objects, people

situations, thoughts, and anything else
Notice whenever you have a judgment about *anything*
And remember to forget what you think you know
Hand over all meaning that you gave the world
and allow in a higher perspective
The mind is naturally abstract
There are no interpretations
that will bring you peace
See all as neutral

~

Judge nothing, you will be happy
Forgive everything, you will be happier
Love everything, you will be happiest
~ Sri Chinmoy ~

Love is the absence of judgment
~ Dalai Lama ~

Judgment is the number one reason we feel blocked,
sad, and alone
~ Gabrielle Bernstein ~

Father, today I leave creation free to be itself.
I honour all its parts, in which I am included.
We are one because each part contains Your memory,
and truth must shine in all of us as one.
~ *A Course in Miracles*, Lesson 243 ~

Know that everything is in perfect order
whether you understand it or not
~ Valerie Satterwhite ~

JUDGE NOTHING
I AM NEUTRAL

Notice Your Reactions

Pause

16

Notice Your Reactions

Pause

If someone says or does something
that you do not like
Do you immediately feel attacked?
Do you attack back without thinking?
If you have a minor accident
Say you spill your drink
Do you immediately shout and curse
thinking, *why me?*

These reactions arise from fearful thoughts
A feeling that the world is against you
but we can always allow space to perceive otherwise
Today we will bring our awareness to these reactions
As always, without judgment

Notice when you are quick to react
Ask yourself whether those reactions
were really necessary
After a few times of noticing your reactions
begin to take a conscious pause
Take a breath
Give it some space
Start responding to life
from a brand-new perspective
You may even find yourself laughing instead!

When you react
you are not really choosing it

it is a programmed effect from a perceived cause

Responding from a place of peace
is always an alternative option
Today we choose peace

~

Responding is based on facts
the present and curiosity
Reactions are based on the past
emotions, and defensiveness
Which one you use
will alter your interactions with others completely
~ *The Joyful Profit Movement* ~

When you react
you are giving away your power
When you respond
you are staying in control of yourself
~ Bob Proctor ~

Respond, don't react
Listen, don't talk
Think, don't assume
~ Raji Lukkoor ~

Accept — then act.
Whatever the present moment contains
accept it as if you had chosen it
Always work with it, not against it…
this will miraculously change your whole life
~ Eckhart Tolle ~

NOTICE YOUR REACTIONS

PAUSE PAUSE PAUSE

Release the Need to be Right

'Truth does not change'

17

Release the Need to be Right

'Truth does not change'

Does it really matter who is wrong
and who is right?
What if no one is right?
What if no one is wrong?
We all experience this world
from different perspectives
different upbringings with different life lessons
Thus, different ideas of what is right and wrong
causing us to feel separate from one another
These ideas can even change multiple times
within one person's lifetime

Whatever can change is not true
but can assist in revealing what is
Today we look beyond the surface
of our varying experiences
to recognizing our shared essence
We are the same in truth

Letting go of the need to be right
assists in healing our belief in separation
Uniting us in the most beautiful way
Giving ourselves permission to be and share
ourselves authentically
without fear of judgment or persecution
We are all on the same journey home
no matter how different that may look

Notice today when you feel a rise inside
to want to prove yourself right
Acknowledge and honor the fact
that your experience varies from others
and ask yourself this question…
Would I rather be right?
Or would I rather be happy?

~

There are only three things you need to let go of
judgment, controlling, and being right
Release these three
and you will have the whole mind
and twinkly heart of a child
~ Hugh Prather ~

Let go of your attachment to being right
and suddenly, your mind is more open
~ Ralph Marston ~

Whenever we release our need to be right
about everything as parents
We can meet our children in a relationship
of mutuality and respect
~ Arjuna Ardagh ~

Do you prefer that you be right or happy?
~ *A Course in Miracles* ~

RELEASE THE NEED TO BE RIGHT

TRUTH DOES NOT CHANGE

Get Comfortable Being Uncomfortable

'I surrender'

18

Get Comfortable Being Uncomfortable

'I surrender'

This may seem completely unnatural
as we have been conditioned to seek comfort
as a way of feeling safe
But what if you knew it *was* safe
to feel uncomfortable?
And what if 'safety'
was actually keeping us feeling stuck
and unfulfilled?

Anything you might think of as uncomfortable
is most likely a lesson gifted to you
A way to show you where you are out of alignment
a signal that you are being guided towards
or on the precipice of something new
or simply just a side effect
of change and growth
You are uncomfortable with what you are not used to
that does not make it bad

Feel into any discomfort today
do not run away or distract yourself
What you resist, persists
so in doing so you are actually holding onto them
All feelings just want to be felt
accept and embrace them
Hold space for them
observe and feel without judgment
and allow them to move through

Listen for the message they may have for you
and say thank you
Feeling is healing
You may be surprised at the genuine comfort
to come from this practice

~

Whatever makes you uncomfortable
is your biggest opportunity for growth
~ Bryant McGill ~

The more time you spend in the discomfort zone
the more your comfort zone will expand
~ Robin Sharma ~

When you become comfortable with uncertainty
infinite possibilities open up in your life
It means fear is no longer a dominant factor
in what you do
and no longer prevents you from taking action
to initiate change
~ Eckhart Tolle ~

We are so successful at being comfortable
that comfort has become the enemy of our success
~ Wim Hof ~

COMFORTABLE DISCOMFORT

I SURRENDER I SURRENDER

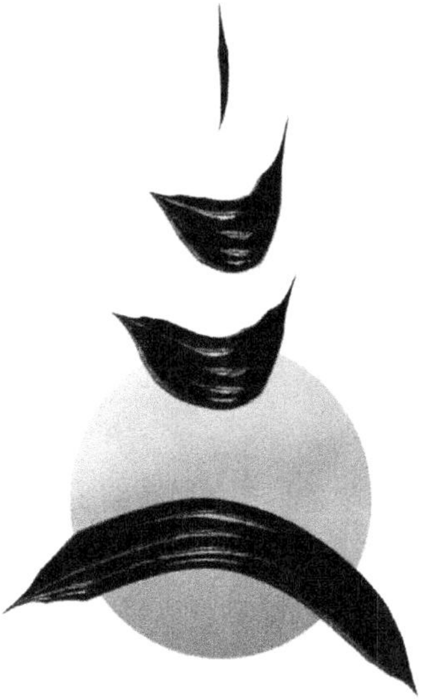

Hello Ego, Goodbye Ego

Ego

19

Hello Ego, Goodbye Ego

Ego

Today we will gently flag any egoic thoughts
simply by noticing them
without judgment or resistance
just by saying to yourself
Ego

Whenever you find you are judging yourself
or anyone else…
Ego
Whenever you're feeling afraid and alone
Ego
Whenever you feel guilt or shame
Ego
Whenever you feel superior or inferior
Ego
Whenever you feel attacked or the need to attack
Ego
Whenever you feel sadness or depression
Ego

By simply becoming aware
of these thoughts and feelings as they come up
and identifying them as the ego
they will begin to lose their power
and control over you
You realize they are not you
You don't have to fight, suppress
or reject these thoughts and feelings

Just look at them, feel them
When you're not looking at the unconscious
you're denying it and projecting it outward
and so it remains held in place
In gently noting to yourself
Ego
You will begin to let it go
as one by one
you place these illusions aside

~

Take no notice of the ego and its activities
but see only the light behind
~ Ramana Maharshi ~

We think that without the ego, all would be chaos
the opposite is true
Without the ego, all would be love
~
The ego is an idea, not a fact
~ *A Course in Miracles* ~

As long as the ego runs your life
most of your thoughts, emotions, and actions
arise from desire and fear
~
Ego is no longer ego when you know there is ego
~ Eckhart Tolle ~

HELLO EGO GOODBYE EGO
EGO EGO EGO EGO

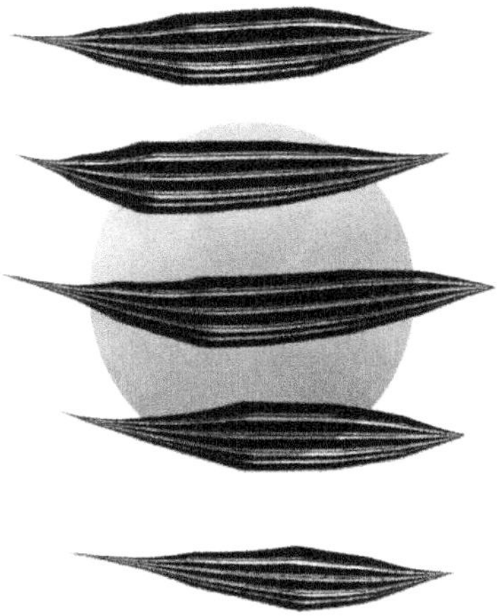

Mantra/Chant down Babylon

Chant

20

Mantra/Chant down Babylon

Chant

To chant a mantra is to take a word
phrase or sound and repeat it
either mentally or vocally
This is a wonderful way to help clear your mind
Giving your thinking mind
something like this to do
leaves little room for compulsive thoughts
and instead fills you up with a higher vibration

Today we will attempt to chant all day
You may find it more practical to chant in your head
but feel free to chant out loud
whenever you feel called

You can look up common mantras for inspiration
or make up your own affirmation
You may repeat your mantra
in rhythm with your breath or heartbeat
sing it along to a tune
or just repeat it at random
Mix it up, make it your own
Choose any mantra or chant
that you feel resonates with you today
and stick with it

When repeating your mantra mentally
Try hearing it rather than saying it
so that it feels light and effortless

Some of my personal favorites include:
Jai Guru… Jai Guru… Jai Guru…
Love… Love… Love… Love…
Forgive... forgive... forgive... forgive
I dedicate all thought to union…
I dedicate all thought to union
I Am… I Am… I Am… I Am
Hong (inhale)… Sau (exhale)… Hong… Sau…
(I am spirit)

~

When you chant 'Aum' or any mantra
do so softly and gently
Extend the sound
Focus your awareness on the sound of the mantra
and become absorbed in it
~ Frederick Lenz ~

Mantra chanting is therapeutic
It energizes the body, purifies the mind
and cleans the soul
~ Fal Rana ~

Chanting opens the heart
and makes love flow within us
~ Swami Muktananda ~

The process of chanting the holy name of the Lord
is so powerful that by this chanting
even householders can very easily gain
the ultimate result
achieved by persons in the renounced order
~ Srimad Bhagavatham ~

MANTRA/CHANT DOWN BABYLON

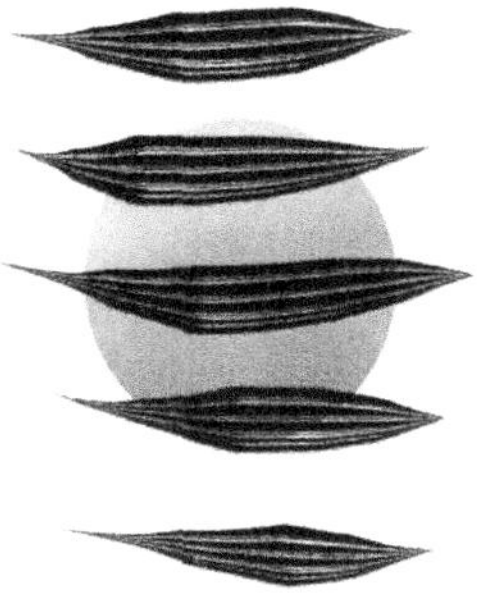

CHANT CHANT CHANT CHANT

Empty to be Filled

Release and recieve

21

Empty to be Filled

Release and receive

Imagine your thoughts as files in a storage box
Notes, essays, images, video clips
all stored up from every experience
you have ever had
creating judgments on yourself
and all that you see
Today we are going to set them free

Visualize the top of your head opening
like a cardboard box
Now imagine all of those files just flying away
drifting off in the breeze
As they do, they gradually dissolve into nothing
You have no use for them now

Notice if you are clinging to anything in particular
try to release judgment
and just enjoy the space you're creating
lifting the weight of the past completely
from your mind

Now we are going to leave that box open
Allowing every moment
to be completely clear of the past
While going about your day today
hold this visualization
of an open, clear storage box
where your brain would be

If you find yourself storing up
any new memories from the day
repeat the beginning exercise and set yourself free
Allow yourself to be filled instead
with divine wisdom
Enter a space of receptivity
Visualize a light flowing down into your box
like sunrays to an open flower
You need do nothing
Just receive, and allow yourself to be filled with Love

~

Empty your cup so that it may be filled:
Become devoid to gain totality
~ Bruce Lee ~

When you're full of yourself, God can't fill you
But when you empty yourself, God has a useful vessel
~ Max Lucado ~

To be filled with the Spirit
we must be emptied of self
~ Unknown ~

Thou must be emptied
of that wherewith thou are full,
That thou mayest be filled.
With that whereof that thou art empty
~ Saint Augustine ~

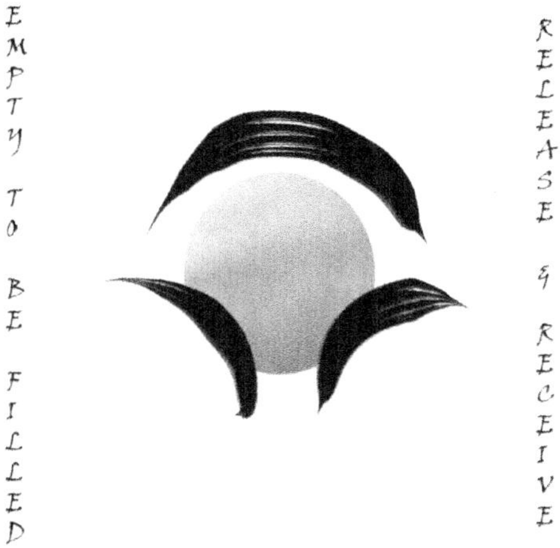
EMPTY TO BE FILLED
RELEASE & RECEIVE

Enter the Portal of the Heart

Listen, feel (heart space)

22

Enter the Portal of the Heart

Listen, feel (heart space)

Tune in to the beating of the heart
You may want to place your hand on your chest
If feeling the beat seems difficult
try holding your breath for a moment
Once you have found it
allow your breath to return to normal
and focus on the rhythm
of your heart beating

The heart space is not only the organ
that we know of in the body
but a central *space*
in which we can connect
with our inner guidance
A portal to our true spacious selves
transcending the form
that we thought ourselves to be
and merging with the light
that embraces all that is

The more we allow ourselves
to connect with and *be* within our heart space
the more open and spacious we begin to feel
In shifting our focus from our thoughts
the mind becomes a clear pool
for the heart's desires to flow through

As often as possible today

bring your attention out of your thinking mind
and seat your consciousness softly
within your heart space

~

The very center of your heart
is where life begins
the most beautiful place on earth
~ Rumi ~

The innermost light
shining peacefully and timelessly in the heart
is the real Guru
All others merely show the way
~ Sri Nisargadatta Maharaj ~

By the practice of meditation
you will find that you are carrying within your heart
a portable paradise
~ Paramhansa Yogananda ~

In the heart of the I-Am person
is the I-Am presence
In the heart of the I-Am presence
Is the absolute
~ Mooji ~

ENTER THE HEART PORTAL

LISTEN FEEL HEART SPACE

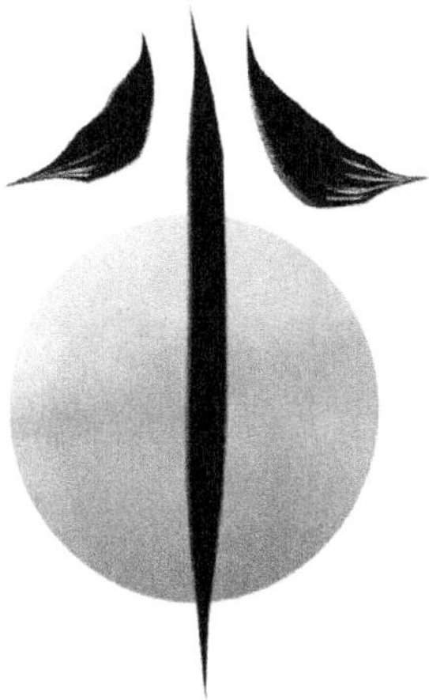

Expect Guidance

Pray, listen, follow

23

Expect Guidance

Pray, listen, follow

Today you will completely free yourself
of making any decisions
How beautiful to have this burden
lifted from your mind
Clear your schedule
and allow yourself to remain open
to receive your inner guidance

Whenever you feel there is a decision to be made
simply hand it over
Imagine this thought rising up to your higher self
and let the decision be made for you
If you practice listening
rather than thinking
you will begin to know what to do

This will take some patience and trust
but will come with greater ease
the more frequently you practice
When in doubt, wait for a sign
Guidance can come in many forms and little nudges
it is always present
there is no need to worry about the future

Go slowly, never rush
or you may miss the signpost
Be open to invitations that are offered to you
Have an awareness of whatever comes your way

as being a potential answer
to what you have been looking for
noticing and releasing any judgment or resistance

Trust that all is as it's meant to be
You are safe
you are loved
you are supported

~

You don't always need a plan
sometimes you just need to breathe, trust
let go and see what happens
~ Mandy Hale ~

If you allow yourself to expect guidance
Guidance will show up
~ Dr. Richard Bartle ~

We listen for guidance everywhere except from within
~ Parker J. Palmer ~

True guidance is like a small torch in a dark forest
It doesn't show everything at once
but gives enough light for the next step to be safe
~ Swami Vivekananda ~

EXPECT GUIDANCE
PRAY LISTEN FOLLOW

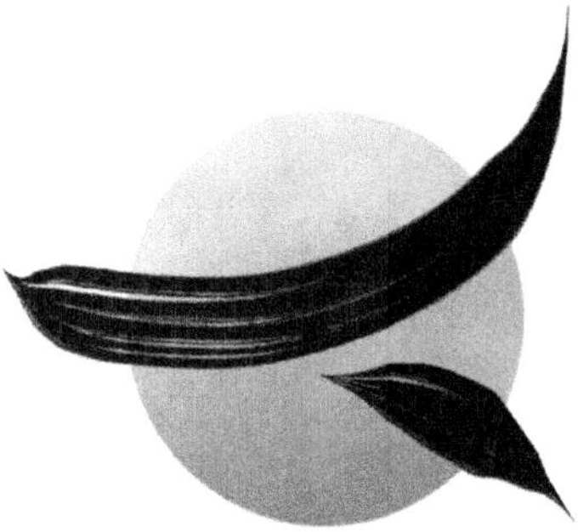

Release Attachment to Outcome

'I release the future'

24

Release Attachment to Outcome

'I release the future'

When we are attached to an outcome
or have certain expectations
we often lose sight of the present moment
Our focus is always set on the future
rather than the process
getting caught in the game of
'once we have done this'
or 'when we do that'
then everything will be perfect
without ever actually reaching that future place

In our minds we are not there yet
then when we are, we skip right past it
In doing so, we are forever delaying the joy
that is actually available to us right now

In having certain expectations
a feeling of disappointment when they are not met
is inevitable
and even if they are met
we are actually placing a limit on what is possible
by projecting the past onto the future

Anything is possible...if you let it be
You cannot control the world you made
but you can release the restrictions
you've tried to put on it

Notice today when you find yourself doing something
while thinking about the pleasure you will feel
when you finish it
Shift your perspective to enjoying the doing
Feel the fullness of life *now*
and release the future to its full potential

~

When you enjoy what you do
work becomes play
~ Martin Yan ~

When you release expectations
you are free to enjoy things for what they are
instead of what you think they should be
~ Mandy Hale ~

Expectation feeds frustration
as it's simply an illusory form of control
by attempting to grip the reins that aren't ours to hold
Breathe, Release. Let go
Allow your life to naturally, quietly unfold
~ Victoria ~

To release others
from the expectations we have of them
is to really love them
~ Shirley Maclaine ~

Expect nothing and accept everything
and you will never be disappointed
~ Lawrence Overmire ~

RELEASE ATTACHMENT TO OUTCOME

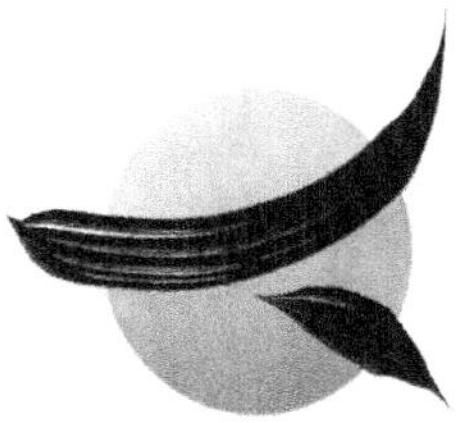

I RELEASE THE FUTURE

Surrender to the Moment

'It is safe to let go'

25

Surrender to the Moment

'It is safe to let go'

Surrender is not giving up on life
but giving up your resistance to it
Relinquishing trying to control the uncontrollable
and allowing yourself to be fully held
by the universe

Completely let go of all concepts
all thoughts, all beliefs
all ideas of who you think you are
that bind you to littleness
and allow yourself to receive the truth

Relax your body, unclench your jaw
drop your guards and breathe a great sigh of release
Trust that you are always taken care of
You have always been *here*
You are already home

As often as possible today
allow yourself to surrender to the moment
Notice when resistance arises
be it to the weather
or the situations you find yourself in
and feel the beauty and the relief
in just letting go
accepting everything as it is

Loosen the hold of all structure

all conformity and restrictions
you have placed upon yourself
and allow your whole being to relax and merge
with the experience that is at hand
You are safe, you are held, you are loved
It is safe to let go

~

The moment of surrender is not when life is over
It's when life begins
~ Marianne Williamson ~

Surrender to what is
Let go of what was
Have faith in what will be
~ Sonia Ricotti ~

Always say 'yes' to the present moment…
Surrender to what is
Say 'yes' to life — and see how life starts suddenly
to start working for you rather than against you
~ Eckhart Tolle ~

Surrender and accept
that whatever is happening at the moment
the universe is working on your behalf
~ Mastin Kipp ~

SURRENDER TO THE MOMENT

IT IS SAFE TO LET GO

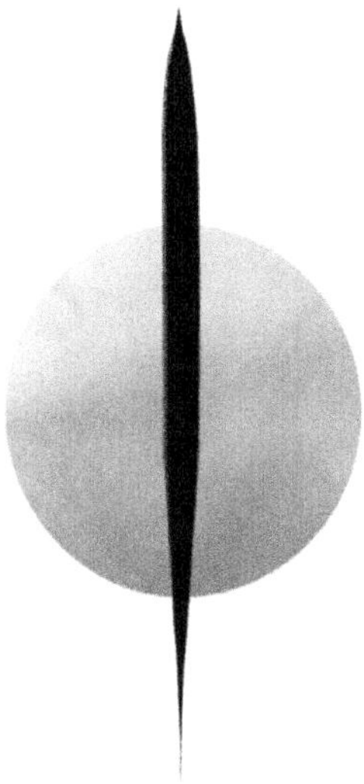

Stay Vertical

'I am the light'

26

Stay Vertical

'I am the light'

Visualize a vertical stream
of white crystal light
shining straight down
from the heavens above
It enters through the crown of your head
traveling down through your entire body
and into the earth
This great ray of light stays with you
wherever you go
there is nothing before or after it
forever present, soft, and still

Being used to horizontal thinking in linear time
this practice will assist in letting this go
recognizing the eternal present moment
in alignment with creation itself
Everything is always happening *now*

As you go through your day
stay present with this light
Visualize it throughout all of your regular activities
When your attention seems to wander through time
gently bring it back to this vertical light
and watch the miracles that unfold
You are here
You are the light

Time is not a linear flow, as we think it is
into past, present, and future
Time is an indivisible whole
a great pool in which all events
are eternally embodied
~ Frank Waters ~

Time is the horizontal dimension of life
the surface layer of reality
then there is the vertical dimension of depth
accessible only through the portal
of the present moment
~ Eckhart Tolle ~

At present, I am light, now I fly
now I see myself below me
now a God dances through me
~ Friedrich Nietzsche ~

Light is to darkness what love is to fear;
in the presence of one the other disappears
~ Marianne Williamson ~

The present moment is the gateway to eternity
~ David Hoffmeister ~

STAY VERTICAL
I AM THE LIGHT

Let Every Moment be Brand New

Fresh eyes

27

Let Every Moment be Brand New

Fresh eyes

Like a newborn baby
or a fresh white page
nothing written upon it
no judgments or opinions, or expectations
no preference or projections from the past
no conditioning, no false beliefs
Let every moment be brand… spanking… new

Greet all that you see
with this fresh, clean perspective
Every person that crosses your path
every little thing that you pass by
don't judge or even label
Everything is new, fresh, reborn
Each seemingly new moment
is completely free from the last
Leaving the future wide open
to infinite possibilities
Undo the *past*
in the present
to release the future

Imagine you were in a virtual reality
exploring alien terrain
in awe of how real everything looks
but knowing it all came from one source
you appreciate the sameness
in all the uniqueness

Become like a child
experiencing everything for the very first time
Interact, play
and be curious about all that you see
as if you had never seen it before
discovering the world anew

~

You have to let yourself be fully present
in every moment
Just be awake for it
do you know what I mean?
Go all in
and wring every last drop out of the experience
~ Jerry Han ~

All that is important is this one moment in movement
Make the moment important
vital, and worth living
Do not let it slip away, unnoticed and unused
~ Martha Graham ~

Every moment is a fresh beginning
~ T. S. Eliot ~

This moment is your miracle
~ David Hoffmeister ~

EVERY MOMENT IS BRAND NEW

FRESH EYES FRESH EYES

See the Light in Everyone

Visualize light

28

See the Light in Everyone

Visualize light

Sit comfortably and take a few deep breaths
relaxing more deeply with every exhale
Bring your attention to your heart center
Visualize a light shining brightly like a star
a steady, constant, brilliant white light
Now feel this light spreading outward
surrounding your entire body
filling the room that you're in
slowly expanding out
into the entire universe

Feel that there is no longer any separation
between yourself and the whole
Close your eyes and sit with this feeling
of pure brilliant radiance for as long as you like
When you're ready, open your eyes

As you go about your daily activities today
remember this light within you
Acknowledge that same light
in every single person you come across
See them as this light only
In this way, you are blessing them truly

See the light shining from the center of their chest
Feel their radiance, their warmth
Whether they outwardly show it or not

Try to release all judgment and thoughts about that person, there are no strangers
everyone is your perfect equal
smile, and just see them as this brilliant light
shining exactly the same way that you do
Bless even those that come to mind
in your thoughts today
with this same recognition
We are the light

~

Love is the recognition of oneness
~ Eckhart Tolle ~

See the light in others
and treat them as if that's all you see
~ Dr. Wayne Dyer ~

Faith is seeing light with your heart
when all your eyes see is darkness
~ Barbara Johnson ~

Nothing can dim the light that shines from within
~ Maya Angelou ~

The same light you see in others,
Is shining within you too
~ Morgan Harper Nichols ~

SEE THE LIGHT IN EVERYONE

VISUALIZE LIGHT

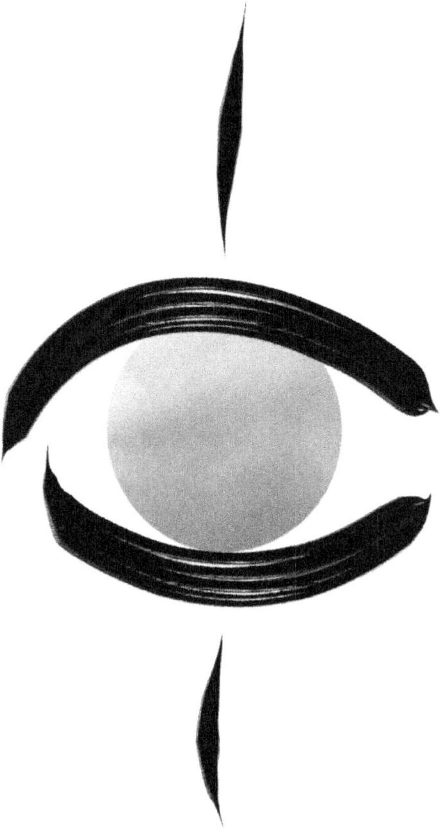

You Are Not the Only One

'I am one'

29

You Are Not the Only One

'I am one'

Today we will acknowledge
that we are not the only one
that experiences life in the way we do
As a human race, we all have struggles
we all experience the same range of emotions
We have all felt separate and alone
in one way or another

At the same time as recognizing
our seemingly separate
yet same experiences
we are not really separate
Deep down we are all longing for the same thing
We desire to *know* Love and be free
and so share the same purpose
to know ourselves fully

If we were all to let go of all of our differing beliefs
separate perspectives and lone experiences
we would recognize what we all are
the exact same conscious awareness
the life behind it all

The presence that is looking through your eyes
is the same presence that looks through mine
Be with this thought
when you look someone in the eyes
as you play hide and seek with yourself

Imagine looking through their eyes
and know that you are the same
There is no separation
You are not the only one
You are one

~

In truth, we are not separate from each other
from the world, from the whole earth
the sun or moon, or billions of stars
not separate from the entire universe
Listening silently in quiet wonderment
without knowing anything
there is just one mysteriously palpitating aliveness
~ Toni Packer ~

You are not separate from the whole
You are one with the sun, the earth, the air
You don't have a life. You are life
~ Eckhart Tolle ~

Surrender means seeing that 'I am not separate'
Just SEEING that 'I am not separate'
Nothing is surrendered, nothing is dropped;
just a nonsense idea
a dream is not more there because you are awake
~ Rajneesh ~

YOU ARE NOT THE ONLY ONE
I AM ONE I AM ONE I AM ONE

No I, No My

Un-label

30

No I, No My

Un-label

This may seem quite challenging at first
but let's have some fun with this today
and attempt this as best we can

One — Let go of the terms I, me, and my
Relinquish the use of any identifications
that suggest that we are a separate being

Two — Let go of descriptive words
that display preference or our personal views
'Likes,' 'dislikes,' and what is 'good' or 'bad'

Try it now to tell me about your morning
You might usually say…
'I woke up late'
'My back was aching badly'
'My partner asked me if I was ok'

In applying today's practice
it might be something like this…
'There was an awakening from sleep'
'A sensation in the back of the body was noticed'
'Words were spoken'

Be as simple as possible in your words
Allow this practice to release you
from your specific judgments
and separate viewpoint

to an expanded state of awareness and peace
Extend this practice to your day
when speaking to people
as well as for your inner commentary
All is… as it is

~

The separate self is like a character in a movie
that travels the world in search of the screen
~ Rupert Spira ~

It is not the person, but the consciousness itself
that wakes up from this mess of a personal existence
When it wakes up, it realizes this so-called mess was
all along Divine
~

What is needed is a good 'I'-wash
a detox from personhood
so that our original being shines unimpeded
~ Mooji ~

There is no such thing as a person
There are only restrictions and limitations
The sum total of these defines the person
The person merely appears to be
like the space within the pot
appears to have the shape and volume
and smell of the pot
~ Nisargadatta Maharaj ~

NO I NO MY

UNLABEL

Forgive the World

Face it, forgive it, and be free

31

Forgive the World

Face it, forgive it, and be free

Today we will be practicing forgiveness
in its highest form
This may seem quite radical
but forgiving *is* forgetting
when we recognize that, in truth
nothing ever actually occurred
overlooking the idea entirely
and removing all of the false meaning that we gave it

Forgiveness is usually seen
as wrongdoing taking place
the victim rising above it and choosing to forgive
But what if it was always *we*
that dreamed the dream we see?
What if we have never been
the victim of our reality?

We could never be alone and apart from the whole
but the ego says we have separated
that we should fear the consequences
the guilt and shame is unbearable
so we push our feelings away
Projecting it all outside of ourselves

Bang

The world we experience is a mirror
of what we believe to be true

reflecting these beliefs back at us
as an opportunity to see
Now we have a choice
Do we believe the impossible
and continue this fearful dream?
Or do we let them all go
and allow the truth to reveal itself

Everyone is another you
How you see another is how you see yourself
When you condemn someone
you are condemning yourself
and thus, keeping yourself bound
by your own judgments
There is no battle out there
There are no opponents
It is all you
In forgiving the world
you are forgiving yourself, forgiving the ego
and thus, setting the world free

All that can change is an illusion
and the truth will always be true
In forgiving every belief as it comes up
Bit by bit, we are healing this illusion of separation
Remembering our holy nature

Notice today, whenever you feel that there is
something wrong in the world
some injustice or reason to fight
When you feel attacked or unfairly treated
or even slightly disturbed
no matter how big or small
Take a deep breath

Recognise you are viewing your own mind
remember the reason you are seeing this outside
is so that you don't have to acknowledge it inside
Forgive what you see
Forgive yourself
In accepting that it is yours
Hold it within the spaciousness of Love
You can choose again
You can break the cycle
Relax and say to yourself
'I forgive this, and I set myself free'
And so it is

~

Fear binds the world
Forgiveness sets it free

~

In complete forgiveness, in which you recognize that
there is nothing to forgive
you are absolved completely

~

Every illusion brought to its forgiveness is gently
overlooked and disappears…
No misery is here, but only joy
~ *A Course in Miracles* ~

Forgiveness… is still, and quietly does nothing…
It merely looks and waits and judges not
~ Kenneth Wapnick ~

FORGIVE THE WORLD

FACE FORGIVE FREE

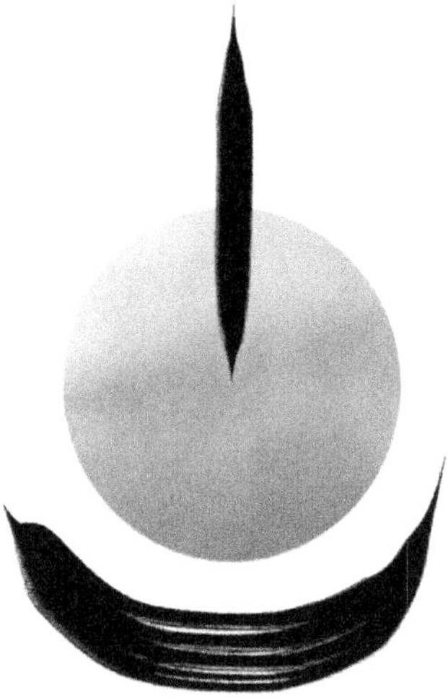

What is your Present Goal

'I am present peace'

32

What is your Present Goal?

'I am present peace'

How are you feeling
in this very moment?
How would you like to feel
in this very moment?
The only way of changing how you feel
is to shift your perception
in this *very moment*

In every moment today
notice how you feel
Whenever you are feeling anything but peace
bring your awareness to whatever it is
that is blocking your peace
Often it is a thought or belief
about the past or the future
A judgment about yourself
a situation or others

Take a breath
Shift your focus to the now
And allow yourself to let it go
Choose again
What do you really want?
We may believe that worldly goals
achieving something outside of ourselves
will bring us what we want
but what if we already have what we want?
And have been hiding it from ourselves

because we feel unworthy

Our present goal is always peace of mind
There is nothing you need to do
but let go of what is blocking it
The past is not here, the future is not here
YOU are here
You are Present Peace

~

How one is feeling now has nothing to do
with an event that happened in history to a body
or with what could happen in the future
How one is feeling
is the result of a present decision of mind
A choice of perception
That, and only that, brings peace or upset
~ David Hoffmeister ~

Realize deeply, that the present moment
is all you ever have
Make the NOW the primary focus of your life
~ Eckhart Tolle ~

Even if you achieve your outer purpose
it will never satisfy you
if you haven't found your inner purpose
which is awakening
being present, being in alignment with life
True power comes out of the presence;
it *is* the presence
~ Eckhart Tolle ~

WHAT IS YOUR PRESENT GOAL

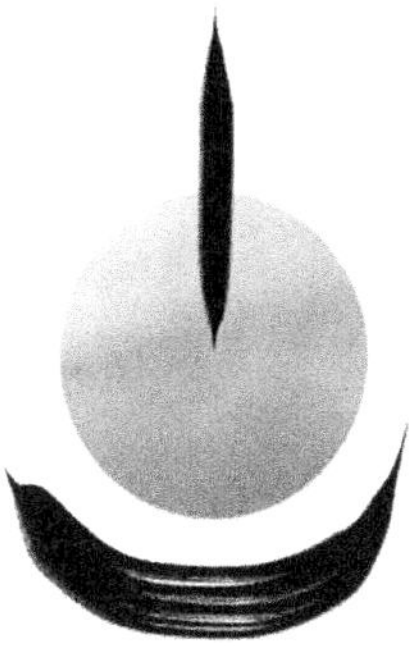

I AM PRESENT PEACE

Follow your Happiness

'I am Joy'

33

Follow your Happiness

'I am joy'

Now that we have established
there is nothing you *need* to do
What would you like to do?
What brings you joy?
What would your favorite activity have been as a child
if you were free to do as you wished?
Connect to the freedom of your spirit
That wants to express itself

Moment by moment, today
follow whatever brings you joy
the calling of your heart
You are allowed to be happy
it is your true function

Release yourself from your regular routines
of what you think you should do
or what you're used to
and try something new
You can start small
walk on the other side of the road
visit a different coffee shop
converse with strangers
go on an adventure
be creative, dance, sing
share your natural gifts
Express and extend the love in your heart
So that it may be felt

by everyone you come across

When you are aligned with joy
you will find it in all things
Let go of the outcomes, and the whys
of what you are doing
if you are in your joy
you are in the right place

~

Just follow your joy… always
I think that if you do that
life will take you on the course it's meant to take you
~ Jonathan Groff ~

Follow your bliss
and the universe will open its doors to you
where there were only walls
~ Joseph Campbell ~

Joy and peace are my inheritance
~
Be happy, for your only function here is happiness
~ *A Course in Miracles* ~

FOLLOW YOUR HAPPINESS
I AM JOY I AM JOY

ABOUT THE AUTHOR

Tyula is another you…
Some may know her as a single mother of two, a kind and loving soul, always calm and ready to welcome you with a smile. Others would have known her as an alcoholic party girl, a nightclub dancer, a weird and wild seductive temptress who spent as much time falling over as she did dancing. Some would say she is a talented artist, a creative costume designer, who specializes in latex and pvc. You may see her as a spiritual teacher, a wise guiding light who has accepted her purpose as a way shower for the great awakening of the world. One might call her a murderer, a liar and a cheat, a selfish b**** who is not to be trusted…
None of these are true. She is another you, making her way back home.

To find out more about Tyula's current offerings, please visit her website – divinereconnection.com or you can find her on instagram @tyularose

Scan QR Code above or visit divinereconnection.com for access to your free downloadable wallpapers to compliment your daily practice.

Choose Love ☺

Printed in Great Britain
by Amazon

26012434R00108